LAYING YOU TO REST

LAUREN EDEN

LAYING YOU TO REST

LAUREN EDEN

LAYING YOU TO REST

Self-published by Lauren Eden
laureneden.me

First edition: 2021

ISBN: 978-0-6489872-1-5

My muse, my ghost.

For turning my pain
into dollar signs.

I knew you would pay
somehow.

FUCKFACE

Son. Cat dad. Ghost. Passed away suddenly from a black heart.

A farewell service will be held in my bedroom (once our bedroom) on 11 April at 9am.

Love of some of my life. My best. Not the rest of it.

GOODBYE

To my dearly beloved dead boyfriend,

Today is your funeral.

I will be laying you to rest under the second she-oak tree on the
left at Pride Park where we shared our first kiss. A sliver of apple
tucked in the left corner of your bottom lip. Juice dribbling down
slowly, like dew from a leaf.

I remember that day I kissed you—the way my tongue had leapt
from my mouth like a pouncing cat, chasing the drop down your
chin as it ran down before it fell, & I thought *that* will be the only
time I will chase this man. *This* might've been the first lie I told
myself about you.

With you, I will be burying all evidence you existed on this
bubble-bursting earth. 1. Our hidden box of drunk & dirty
Polaroids. 2. The silver-plated promise ring with the citrine
crystal that broke & you never returned—just like the rest of your
promises. 3. The clothes you left behind unwashed in the
laundry hamper. (I am not your mother. If I was, I would've
taught you better manners). 4. Your stash of Gummy Bears &
other childish snacks you insisted needed to be presented upon
their own shelf, like a collection of Transformers clinging to your
boyhood with whiter knuckles than you ever clung to me.

And lastly, I will sprinkle that last sprig of hope I have kept until
now; folding each corner of us slowly, like a love note, in the way
we deserved. I know it's the 21st century baby, but you know I
am old school. I still keep a diary. I still reach for a pen to write
a number on the back of my hand. You must understand that
love is not an atomic bomb. We cannot be erased by a few simple

taps on a phone screen—it is not the way I close. And I absolutely, desperately, sure as hell need to close.

Respectfully not yours,

Me

P.S. They keep telling me you're not really dead, though to me that is dubious, & I don't care to split the hairs I've pulled from my head waiting for you to return to me. I'd rather just settle it now. You really are, very much, almost dead to me.

CHAPTERS

I   SEE YOU TONIGHT

BACK ON THE SHELF

The first time I borrowed
a book from the library
I found out that worlds
were only on loan to me
before I had to give them
back.

My fingerprints might
be all over your spine,
but your barcode spells:
You are not mine.

WONDERLAND

You were a disaster,
& I was flirting with you.

Still, I was no do-good nurse.
I had the curse of the siren
with the voice of a husky-voiced bar singer
that prompted men to ask for a light.
Men like to think they can tell
a girl's worst habit just by looking at her,
& not by what she's looking at.
But I can tell you boy, she's looking at you.

"I don't smoke," I said, when you asked.
     "I flame."

You asked for my name. I lied. "Alice."
I held out my hand. "Welcome to Wonderland."

You bought me a drink & I took the first sip,
capsized by your sea anchor smile.
I never wondered whether your
double-shot love potion was going to make me feel
ten feet tall in your rabbit-hole pupils,
or cut me down to size.

I already knew by the way you leaned in:
torso tilted forward, gaze shifted to the left of me,
like a message lost in translation that said:
Baby, I'm right here, while looking out the window.
It was going to be both.

TENTH

Your fuck-eyes
glow like a cat's
in the heat of
the night

& I am frightened
(slightly) by the hint
of your hand on my
lower back that arches
in instinct for you to
saunter through like
marble: expensive
but durable enough
to stand all my nine
lives

but there is something
about the way you pull
the skin clean off my
bones with your teeth
that tells me you might be
my tenth.

YOU

Some nights
I wear nothing but
the thought of you,
& I am breathtaking.

DRUNK

Your hands creep up my skirt
before the sand does. A pitter-patter
of fingertips, like rain, ignoring the plea
to come again another day.

Legs as long as summer tides
fold under me like a deck chair.
My skin, salt-shaken but unstirred,
as my melon-martini flavoured tongue
sips the last words out of you,
ending in one long surprise slurp—*I-love-you.*
Your confession burst open on my tongue
like sherbet-filled candy, sickly sweet.

"I love you, too," I reply with a smile.
Your hands rise with the sea.
You are drunk.
That boy is drunk.

God, would you look at that?
That boy is drunk on me.

THE CLEAREST EYE

Real love isn't a blur.
Not a drunken fall.
Not a slow song in a dance hall
in an 80's John Hughes movie
about a clumsy teen
tripping
in the too-big-to-fill heels
of Aphrodite.

It isn't a red rose petal fantasy.
Not a night in a fancy hotel suite
with a whisper of forever on a top-floor
balcony of stars winking at you,
as though you are their wish.

Real love is the clearest eye.
It is the universe seen
through a single drop of dew.
Its crisp edges glistening,
feathering to a dream.

It is the honest pupil centring,
pinning itself to a lover
like a bullseye, while the world
wildly waves its red flags.
Blinking once, the eye sees
only light.

DOLLHOUSE

Mornings with you:
our two shoulders bumping
like moons in our too-tiny bathroom.
Competing to spit first
in our one too-tiny sink.

"It's cute," I'd told you before we moved in.
        "Quaint. Like a dollhouse."
Setting the perfect plastic scene,
the model Mattel mirage
ending with an engagement ring we'd live inside
like mice, spinning circles around each other till we died.

"I guess I am your toy-boy," you agreed.
        "You are three months older than me."

I thought of the box of Ken doll heads
I'd stashed under my bed when I was a little girl,
their heads popped from their necks like zits
I could never seem to resist the urge to squeeze.
I guess you could say I've always had
a strained relationship with men.

I smiled at you, keeping tight-lipped
on my long & sordid never-*Ever After*
fairytale history. You bumped me out
of the way playfully.

I could think of worse things in life
than spending my mornings
bumping into you.

HALLELUJAH

You tucked my hair
behind my ears
then kissed me.

First on my forehead
second on my lips
third on my left cheek
fourth on my right.

A sign of the cross
you told me meant:
Hallelujah for you.

"See you tonight."

II   THE VERY MISSING PERSON

ALL ON THE TABLE

Whistling a sunny tune.
Hair wound in a top knot,
like a doorknob opening into a portal
of 1950's housewife dreams.

Vermillion red lipstick kissed.
Miles Davis *Blue in Green.*
Sylvan frilly apron I will keep on
for dessert. Duh, I'm dessert.

I've always been a lousy cook.
Spices—I get them more mixed up
than algebra & trigonometry.
More than simile & metaphor.
More than virtues & vices.
Ginger on beef, parsley on lamb,
turmeric through rice.
Must be because I'm sugar, babe
& all those other things nice.

Tripping over the cat circling
figure eights between my legs,
I do the math: It's eight.
You're late.

Wrapping your dinner in foil,
I cover a growing yawn.
Walk into our walk-in robe.
Half your clothes are gone.

WORRYWART

She is right.
I am a worrywart.

Come to think of it,
I'm not sure I've made
anything in life
look more natural
than worrying.

I'm the type of girl
that turns a sore tummy
into a burst appendix.

I'm the type of friend
that turns an unanswered call
into a homicide.

I'm the type of girlfriend
that when her boyfriend texts:
I'm going to be tied up at work,
I'll reply: *By whom?*

PERFECT

"Did you two have a fight?"
      your mum pries.

"No. We were perfect."

Perfect.
I feel the word drip slowly
from my mouth like a snowflake,
freefalling into my open palm.
I study its design.
Its one of a kind webbing,
inimitable by any other code.

Perfect. Perfect. Perfect.
I repeat the word, hypnotised.
The likeness like effigies
in a snowstorm charade.
The murmur of my mouth,
a pottery wheel, whirring
till they change shape on my tongue.

We were perfect. *Perfect.*

The word melts in my hand.
Not in my mouth.

RADIO NOISE

White lies we slip to our lovers like pills:
the topic on breakfast radio
offering reconciliation to
the listening morning commuters
with lipstick on their white collars.

First caller: a henpecked husband
confessing to taking a week off work
without telling his wife
to tee off at the golf course
during business hours.
I rolled my eyes.
If this is as juicy as middle-age gets,
then drug me with lies.

Each morning, he explained,
he'd get up at the usual time,
put on his shirt & tie, kiss his wife—
all while keeping his face
straighter than his golf swing.
"Have a good day at work," she'd call.
He'd wave goodbye. Do a U-turn
at the next street.

But she was lucky.
At least her lover still came home each night.
Even if it was with his lies stuffed deep
inside his pockets, like a folded note
with the number of a girl,
that was most definitely not
his wife's.

THE ESCAPE ROUTE

She apologises first,
like she's calling in sick for you:
a twenty-six-year-old relationship-apprentice
claiming stress leave.

"I'm sorry honey, but he said he's not coming home."
    "Well when do you expect he might be in?" I say,
like a cold caller trying to get a little warmer.

"He's confused. He needs room to breathe. *Space.*"
    "Couldn't he have just opened a window?
Why'd he have to sneak out the backdoor?"

She begins telling me her favourite story of you.
That time you tried to run away from home when
you were only two. She thinks it defines you.
"Even packed his toothbrush," she says, proudly. "He's
    just like his dad. The moment smoke appears
he's out."

"No. He isn't like that. He hated that about his dad.
    Maybe we should file a missing person report."

"He's not missing.
    He doesn't want to come home."

SPACE

Space. You need space.

More than those stars of sweat
glittering like webs across my chest?

More than those cosmic eyes
blinking at you like lighthouses,
granting your every wish
from vacation to dinner to sex position?

More than that warm, wet galaxy
between my legs?
More than that universe of love,
like an abyss, you could never touch
the bottom of?

You don't know space.
You are the dark matter.

Space junk crashing to Earth like bombs.
A black hole, like an open mouth, guzzling light.
A moonwalker with glow-in-the-dark star
stickers across your bedroom ceiling,
trying to conquer me with your flag
down your *Star Wars* pyjama pants.

But it was all a hoax.
You never landed on me.

The only stake you claimed
was the one you burned me to.

CRYPTIC

I think about putting your face
on the back of a milk carton.

Maybe on the label
of your favourite beer.

The brand of ale your mates drink.
Their fingers peeling
your *Missing Person* notice
absently between sips
as though it were a pair
of girl's knickers.

I imagine you all sitting together
watching the football,
making jokes
about how a girl like me
can't take a hint.

But this was not a crossword of easy clues.
This was something serious.
This was cryptic.

MISSING

Appearance: 5'11. He'll argue 6ft if you find him. Has one sad eye, one happy eye. Has a voice that will make you want to take your pants off. Date of disappearance: March 30. Last seen: In my arms. Tends to walk on the roads less traveled i.e. outside Google Maps range.

III YOU LOOK LIKE YOU'VE
SEEN A GHOST

R U OK BABY?

Ten missed calls.
Seven unanswered text messages.
Three voicemail recordings.
One drawn-out dial tone
like a dark tunnel
echoing
with the beat of
my door-knock heart.

A call cut short,
like an umbilical cord,
& you running off with the baby.
Our baby.

"This was my love too!" I want to shout.
The love you threw away.
I just feel you ought to had given me
some notice somehow,
like, "Baby, I'm putting us on the kerb
      in two days."

But people always take love away,
like it was only ever theirs.

SOUR MILK

You tried to break up with me
the morning of my cousin's wedding
last Spring. We both know you would fall
just short of committing murder
if it got you out of going to a wedding.

I remember us sitting stiff-bodied at the service.
Our two cold bums on the church pew
as I tried not to cry. My eyes puffy like sores
as I blamed it on sentimentality.

The telltale difference between
a happy cry & a sad cry
is that for only one of them
you reach for a Kleenex.

Grimacing at all that *until-death-do-us-part*
optimism, I'd tried to peel your fingers
from my hand like stickers
as you clamped on for dear life.
You had not been a good enough boy
to deserve those.

The next day, I blamed it on the weather.
That strange weather at weddings forecast
the moment the invitation arrives in the mail
& pinned to the refrigerator three months in advance,
like a neon sign: *Not Us*
flashing every time you reach for the goddamned milk.
Even though you know you're just being sour.

SANDMAN

"You are the heaviest sleeper I've ever known,"
    you'd once said. "Like a freight train
at the railyard.
    You just don't move."

"It's trust," I'd answered simply.
    "I don't need to sleep with
one eye open with you."

I should've slept with two open.

SLEEPING DOGS

Let sleeping dogs lie, they say.
Let them wake up to the truth, too.
Which one sleeps more sound? —
The noise of reason,
or the symphony of silence?

I find no grace in it.
Silence is revenge
served on an empty dinner plate.

I lick for clues. I let every woman text for me.
Anger: *I gave one fuck. Two fucks. Three fucks. Four.
  Five fucks. Six fucks. Seven fucks. No more.*
Love: *Baby, your love was genius. Maybe I just didn't
  understand it.*
Pride: *I have no need for revenge. I am no longer yours,
  & that is punishment enough.*

It's futile. Nagging women
only remind you of your mother,
& that helpless state of infancy
you thrash out of loving arms to conquer.

The more I begged the harder you kicked me
with that great big invisible combat boot, winding me.
I begged until I could no longer recognise myself.
I begged until I was no longer begging you for love,
but begging you for mercy,
& even though I knew that silence was your answer,
just as the unsaid presence of an empty sky is,
I still needed to hear the whispers,

the workings out,
your algebraic intentions—
even if I might never understand them.

I still needed to know. *Please.*
How did your heart talk you out of me?

PRIVATE ID

I count five rings before you answer,
the way a child counts his toes.

"Hello?"
You are alive.
    "Who's this?"
My heart drops like my phone.
Only one of them is caught.

"Your girlfriend. Remember? You have a *girlfriend.*"

There is rambling. A lot of it.
Mumbles about life & not knowing what is real.
Crumbs of excuses fall in my hands. I peck for clues.
Expectations. Lost. A break. Space.
I let you mumble on like soft cream
before interrupting sharply, like a knife,
cutting to the chase.

"I'm not going to hear from you again, am I?"
    You pause. "Of course you will."

I hang up the phone without reply,
put on my rock star glasses & watch
our relationship flash before my eyes
like a camera shutter. The pain-paparazzi
publishing your famous last words
on my heart: *Of course you will.*

CRASH. TESTED. DUMMY.

I am the butt of jokes.
Index finger to thumb.
Flicked out of your life like a cigarette
while you kept driving;
our dreams whizzing by
in a faded blur of streetlights.

For three years I played shotgun,
& you, the silver bullet. Appeasing
the motion sickness I trusted you
to navigate yourself out of.
But you were a shit driver—
losing a brownie point for every demerit.
Our relationship hitting brick walls.
Crash. Tested. Dummy.

Don't tell me you didn't know
you hadn't done anything wrong.
Speeding away quickly
so you didn't have to watch me bleed.

Men who aren't guilty
don't run out on women
like they are fleeing a crime scene.

You killed me to save yourself.
That extra breath you have now in your mouth—
how does my life taste?

THAT SHADE OF BLUE

I know it clearer than that
shade of blue in your eyes.

More crystal
than that glacial glint,
like an ice cube
clinking
at the bottom
of a whiskey glass.
You're not coming back.

More alarmingly
than those two barrel-gun pupils
I'd once fall upon my knees
in surrender to,
begging to be spared
from your sniper sight.
You're not coming back.

You see,
that kind of blue doesn't lie,
& it certainly doesn't tell the truth
either.

WEASEL

"I've never heard you cry like that before."

Low animal moan
on all fours. Sobbing
on the bathroom floor.
My final roar.

Purging you like snake venom.
Like an exorcism.
Emptying myself of you,
like a birth. But through the mouth.

Only I knew for certain,
this time,
you weren't coming out alive.

MAGGOTED

The fly buzzes in the room
like a mechanical drone
sending pictures to you.

A silver space-suited astronaut
landing on the moony flesh
of my stomach, as I lie there
watching
his small twitching legs
splay against my arm
the way you'd bend mine
over the edge of the bed.

The fly knows I am dead.
He lands on my nose.
A small gesture letting me know
he's keeping my secret safe.

But I nose, he says.
I nose. I nose. I nose.

MARCO POLO

Marco Polo, I see you.
A blindfold over your eyes.
My underwear stuffed in your mouth.
Calling to me muffled
with your long arms reaching out.

I see you moving on
in the only way you know how:
pretending not to see me,
pretending I don't exist.
Your blind eye closing,
changing from your left to your right
like traffic lights
conducting the pedestrian flow of guilt
that walks across your mind.

I know your strategy, Marco Polo.
I wear no blindfold.
I see right through you.

I know
that if the only way for you to move on
was to close your eyes
& feel your way through the dark,
that it is me you're bumping into
at every corner.

HOOPER HUMPER-THAT'S-WHAT-YOU-THINK

I dreamt you returned to me,
rain-soaked & cold
on a Sunday afternoon.

If it had been a Tuesday, I might've felt differently.
It's too easy to feel lonely on a Sunday.

You stood there in the doorway.
A smirk on your face.
A bouquet of jasmine in your hands.
Your rucksack tucked between your legs
like a tail. Sniffing for a compliment.
Circling for a bone.
I'd already pointed one at you.

Taking one look at my arms folded across
my chest, you'd sighed—
expecting they'd be open.
Did you expect a balloon, too?
A sign that said *Welcome Home*?
A Hallmark card with teddy bears & a quip?
A drink in your hand?

You must understand a girl can only do so much,
& "Baby," I said,
my hand disappearing through you like a ghost,
      "I'm still exhausted from having to organise
your search party."

FOOTPRINT PATTERN ANALYST

I study the pattern of your footprints.
The length of your stride.
The distance they travelled.
Those fine white lines, like branches,
leading to riper fruit. Did she taste
like peach or fig?

I analyse your escape on foot.
The orb of your heel like a smooth half-moon,
ballet light in touch—not scuffed, not smudged.
Clearly no one dragged you by them
to the cheap hotel you checked in. Dirty swipe card
lighting up to your arrival, like her eyes
as she laid on the bed in a lovely spread.
Such a gracious hostess.
Me, kneeling in the dirt with my magnifying glass
like a sexless Nancy Drew, looking for clues
in my faded blue jeans. Raglan tee.
My look: Girl Next Door. Without the doorbell.
Without the *Welcome* mat.

If you ever come back to me,
you know it would be foolish of me
to let you back in so easily.
Not when I could've sworn I had
the huntsman at my door,
& not the wolf.

CHECKMATE YA LATER

They climbed out through the holes in your story.
Pairs & pairs of long, long legs
like spiders
creeping from the trapdoors
under your bed. You, stuck inside
your labyrinth of lies like a sticky web.
Stupid fly.

You'd always said I reminded you of a spider.
Alluring. Elegant gait. Mind, intricate like a web.
You never guessed I was the black widow.
Steel wire web around your neck—caught out in your games.
I was always more competitive than you.
Never sold my property portfolio in *Monopoly*.
Studied obscure three-letter words for *Scrabble*.
I pinned the tail on you, ass.

But there's one vital step missing in your story
that stops it from making sense.
If you have ghosted me—that means you're dead.

But I haven't killed you. Yet.

IV   KILLING YOU

9 - D U M B - F U C K

With lowball tactics, I hit you where it hurts.
Hunt you down again on private caller ID: The Grim Reaper.
Ring, ring. Death is calling.
Death comes best dressed in leather
with a head full of curls,
& unlucky for you,
those killer long eleven legs.

Your black oversized hoodie.
Lace lingerie beneath.
666 is one sexy beast.

This time you don't answer.
I get in my car. I drive to your work.
The jangle of my keys play a heavy metal symphony
conducted in my hand.
Are you ready to rock?
Heads are gonna roll.

You're back from vacation.
Crack! Your suntanned face returns to white
like a whip. Surprise!
You look like you've seen a ghost.
Like I'm the ghost.

"Liar. Coward."
I throw insults at your head like knives.
You duck.
Looking at me like you don't know
what the fuck I'm talking about.
I know that look well.
You never knew what I was talking about.

I roll my eyes.
Push my bra up high.
My breasts spill over like milk.
Just enough to make you want to cry.

I point my index finger at your head & say,
    "Bang. Fucking bang."

PARTING GIFT

Your final parting gift
was the way you broke up with me.

You couldn't have made it
any easier to get over you.

DRAMA KING

You always thought your hurt was bigger than everybody else's,
just because you'd put it where we all could see it:
drinking it/smoking it/fucking it away.
But there was never anything small,
never anything quiet about ours.

Your pain was the centrepiece.
The vase of dead roses we'd all gather around
to talk about your thorns.
Tucking in our own sadness,
like a napkin we'd wipe our mouths clean with
to talk to you about you.
How can we be of service?
How can we devote our lives to you, Drama King?
Fighting not to choke on our bitterness,
as we'd smooth our cutting words on the insides
of our cheeks to deliver polished gems of encouragement
the way the doctor ordered; our faces in varying shades of green
with the grim diagnosis: when one is sick, we all get sick.

Every Friday night, I would wait
for your words to slur. Wait for you to tell me
the same philosophical monologue on repeat at 2am,
while I yawned & pretended you were clever.
Losing you in the beer/the pipes/the white lines,
as you'd disappear in your own puff of smoke
like a magician. The magic word *Sorry*
bringing you back
to my bed/my lips/my life—
until next time.

DARK SIDE

You knew what he was like,
they argue,

& yes,
that is true.
I cannot argue
I wasn't acquainted
with your dark side.

It's just that when you held my hand,
you always held it on your light.

V I HAVE SOMETHING IN MY EYE

MIRAGE

They all look better when we miss them.

No one sees clearly with
tears in their eyes.

THE FEAR INSTINCT

It was like that feeling of panic
you get on the edge of sleep
when you think you're about
to fall out of bed
when you're smack
in the middle.

You would hold my
hand & all I could see
were the ends of your fingertips
where I'd someday

fall.

MOON HOAX

I am spiraling away from you—
in the same resolute circles
I'd once spun around you.

In blue cotton flirt eyes.
In raspberry red O mouths.
Like the opening of a womb. A tunnel.
A black hole. To somewhere else.
To someone else's bed/picture frame/wedding
plus-one invitation.

For three years I landed on
your blue planet eyes.
My heart aged in six.

I cannot catch my breath in grief.
I wear a space helmet: a clear
plastic film between the memory of your
kiss & the promise of another's,
preserving myself in a bubble untouched,
like the bed of a dead child
lined with a horizon of stuffed teddies,
feeding the illusion
that life is closer than it appears.

I am spiraling,
spiraling away from you.
There is no gravity in grief.
There is no gravity in grief.

No stars to hold onto.
No crescent moon, like a hook,
to keep me still. No light.

No string theory to tie us back together.

Like a theory, we were.
Declared. Never proven.

GRAND SADNESS

It was a grand sadness.
The kind
where all the little niggling aches
you'd folded up inside
the corners of your heart
drop to their knees
to pay respect.

Pain doesn't know it's small.
Not until something bigger than itself
tells it so.

THE WEIGHT OF THINGS

I miss you.
I love you.
I need you.

The softest words, like feathers.
Like bricks in the wrong hands.

COLD FEET

I became *the cool girlfriend*
picking you up from city bars at 4am.
Arriving to a pretty girl playing nurse to you
as you sat there on the kerb looking up at me coyly
through the gaps of your fingers
like a petty criminal.

I became *the no-questions-asked girlfriend*
pretending not to notice every time you'd take
your phone into the bathroom,
or lay it face down on the bed,
like a girl you were fucking
that you were ashamed to be fucking.

The it-happens girlfriend
excusing each time you'd fall limp inside me
like a kitten with no roar.
Like a soft lick settled dumbly
in the inside of my cheek.

But you needed the friction.
The chaos of wood against leather.
The rip of sharp words against silk negligees.
That's when you would go out for things:
things that weren't me. That's how I knew
you would always fuck things up,
no matter how good you had it.

No matter how warm the bed was,
you would always sleep with your feet out.

I WILL BURY YOU

"I'm going to bury him," I said,
staring at the picture of you
propped lopsided on the mantle—
barely a leg to stand on.

"Get him. He deserves all the shit coming to him
        after what he's done to you."

"I'm not talking about revenge. I mean it.
        I need to bury him. I need to lay him to rest."

A funeral to farewell a lover
passing from one heart & into another's.
Love buried in a closed casket
unable to be opened
from the inside-knowledge of my soft spots.
A ritual to keep me on the good side of the bitter line.
Gratefulness is greener on the other side.

You meant this much to me.
Look at these flowers.
Listen to this music I've chosen.
Look how much I loved you.

VI   TURNING YOU INTO A NICER
     PERSON THAN YOU WERE

HAUNTING ENGAGEMENTS

With heart i's & scented markers,
I invited you to your own funeral.

I couldn't imagine what kind of prior
haunting engagements a ghost might have
paramount to attending his own funeral.
It is the ultimate fly-on-the-wall experience.
What did these people think of me?

It isn't an empty invitation.
A goodwill-gesture.
The kind where you bump into
an old friend at the supermarket,
calling out as you walk down
different aisles, "Coffee soon? I'll call you!"

Though it could be argued
it is an impossible proposition.
But nothing seemed impossible for you.
Just us.

THE SPIDER & THE FLY

I will meet you in the middle & miss you there.
In the succulent fleshy middle of us.
In the sweet tender meat of our love.
We were the gravy, baby.

Pull up a chair & sit down
before the hurt creeps back in
sneakily
like a spider
who abandoned her web
once her belly was full.

Recognising that
sometimes it is the spider
that feels trapped
in the very web she weaves.

KEEP CALM & EMBALM

Like grapes grown from the vine of your lies,
I collect my dreams from you. One by one
unhooking them from your rhubarb mouth.
Picking them from your hair where I'd braided them
in your sleep. Gouge them from the empty barrel
of your chest—I swear I could've heard one scream.
And held them. Every silken one of them.

My dream of walking down the aisle to you
wearing a dress of sea-blue.
Not white like the tide.
You went deeper than that in me.
I was 20,000 leagues in love with you.

Our dream of the cabin in American northlands
with broken wooden planks & air so damp
our washing never dried. An acoustic guitar
taking shifts in your arms. Rustic paint-spattered floors
papered with first-draft poetry
& love making itself on command.

The dream in our biology:
making a boy & girl in our likenesses.
Long kisses in the kitchen with watching eyes & groans,
& other cliché happy-couple ideals
clinging to hope—
tubes snatched from their noses.

Breathing them in one last time,
in one long breath,
I blew my wishes back out again
like thorn, scattering
back to the dandelion.

LACONIA

My god. Do you look like one.
Lying there bathed in woody-scented
perfumes & olive oil. Your rough edges
softening from a pointy star to a moon.
Your sharp mind bending like a spoon.
Magic happens in water. That embryonic state
where only love can enter.

I wipe your father from your brow.
Your mother from your eyes like sleep.
How much of you was you?
How much of you was them?
Everything that broke your heart
broke mine in the end.

I hold your feet in prayer,
honouring the nomad in your soles.
Scrubbing that restless instinct in you
to wander & wonder
of that green grass on the other side—
the weed: the only thing that could make you settle.
Your soul always niggling, like a stone at the bottom of a sock.
The skin between us getting in the way of us.
Rubbing together like bone on bone.
Wanting to cause damage.
Your moon in Scorpio.

I drop your hand in the water.
I let go of you.
Watch your fingers separate like wild reeds,
with my reflection
blurred
between them.

JACK-SHIT & JILL

Lips, ruby at your neck.
Tongue lashing fire. I test
the temperature
of your Adam's apple
pie before taking a bite.

Like a bee siphons nectar, I drain you
of blood. Replace you with honey.
I can only wish you had been made
of something quite so sweet.

Inside you the bees would make circles.
Not hexagons. Tiny pinpricks of light
dizzying in you
the way I loved you like a child
spinning in the long grass
until I fell down. Rolling down the hill
with the pungent smell of vinegar up my nose,
brown paper in my hands & pen,
& you, with the broken head.

EYE SHUTTERS

"I like the way your eyes move in your head."

You pulled a face at me.
Always thinking my compliments were strange.
They'd never hire me at Hallmark.

"Like a sparrow darting its head robotically looking for crumbs.
      I think your eyes must be square."
You rolled your eyes at me.

I pull down your eyelids like shutters
to the memory, remembering how
you'd always squint when you looked at me,
as though you could never seem
to quite make me out.

Now I know that I was just too bright for you.
Last night I walked home from the bar
linking arms with the moon. Darkness thrown over
my shoulder like a cardigan
in case the cold came, but it never did.
The cold was you.

VENTRILOQUIST

With thread, I sew your mouth shut.
Corner to corner. Enji red.
Though I suspect I didn't need to.
Your lips were shut so tightly in the end
not one pretty-penny thought could
escape them. But first, I am a ventriloquist,
putting words in your mouth,
like balls in the open mouth
of a fairground clown:

I'm sorry.
It wasn't your fault.
I just got tired.

I write your goodbye note with a Sharpie pen,
thinking about the time I argued with you
that no one would distinguish a Sharpie-branded pen
from a regular no-name black marker,
just from looking at a drawn line.
You argued otherwise.
Insisting quality can always be defined.

Maybe that's all it was:
you'd replaced me with a cheaper brand.
A clone of me with a simpler head.
One of those digestible girls
like crumbs
broken from a woman
bigger than your mouth could chew.

PYROMANIAC

Behind the eight ball
the black widow loses
an eye.

Onyx black, your heart,
blinking
as my hand closes over
like an eyelid.

Treasure pried from an open chest.
Certified junk.
Strings of intestines, like pearls,
hanging from a fallen king.

I scrape the charred edges of
your heart like burnt toast.
Did you stand too close to the furnace?
Did you play with too much fire?

My reckless little firebug,
lighting fires in me
then leaving; ash stained on your sleeve:
a charcoal X
where your heart used to be.

VII   IT'S YOUR FUNERAL

9 A M

I am burying you today with the weeds & the thorns.
I'm keeping the roses.

Eleven days into the fourth month.
You always liked your numbers.
Your mystical signs.
Fibonacci.
This time, yours is up.

9am. Bring a flower, I'd said.
My underwear in your pocket.
Wear blue.

I never heard from you.

BLACK CAT

I put on that black velvet bodysuit
you said made me look like a cat.

One you'd cross the street to avoid
if you saw coming.
Your bad luck. Your karma.

Whipped a flash of red across my lips
like a warning. *Oh, the drama.*
Slipped into black leather
like an ink blot
rebelling against cursive.

Six-inch heels. Blade thin.
The kind that gave you a complex.

Black lace veil across my eyes.
A widow before a bride.

BLUE

We are gathered here today
to talk about you
in ways we may not all agree upon.

Like a kaleidoscope,
each of us experienced only
one pattern
one experience
one image
one version of you—
& me?

I liked myself best with you.
I fear I dislike the rest.

They say truth is only one version of things.
All I know is you were blue.
Blue when you looked at me.

When you looked out at the world
you were green
& when the world looked back
you were yellow.

But all I care for is blue.
Blue when you looked at me.

A-MEAN-BOY RHAPSODY

Let me paint a picture of you.
Before you spat on it.

Your colours swirling into an oil slick,
like an eddy of psychedelic pain
I slipped in.

Your mind was the temple I sat in
cross-legged & awed. Your stained-glass window
eyes filled with pictures of far-flung idols & tragedy.

You were brilliant, but sad. Always sad.
Like a blue moon happening once
& not again. But of course this isn't true.
It's just sometimes we only remember the once:
the first time a dream walks up to you on two legs
& kisses you awake.

But it was your mind I was in love with.
The mind I mistook for your heart.
Your wild ideas, like horses,
running untamed rings around us both.
Everybody else was dull.
Everybody else I'd heard before.
You opened your mouth & new planets fell out.

It was your mind I was in love with.
The mind I mistook for your heart.
Like two apples—one covered in toffee.
My tongue stuck on only one half of you.

I loved you. I loved you. I loved you.
The picture I painted of you.

My muse, my art.
I'm sorry for not seeing
your heart.

ON YOUR KNEES, BOY

You will not get me down on my knees
to say the last prayer.

Instead I will remember you on yours.
Mouth crushed between my legs, like a flower.
A string of drool like rosary beads.
Each lick a prayer.
Worshipping at the altar of my body
like it just might save you.

"*God*," you'd say,
        over & over between mouthfuls of me.
God. God. God.

And at the time I thought
you were talking to the heavens,
but now I know
you were talking to me.

PAUL-BEARERS

It took three men to carry you out of my life
& take your place. I am not ashamed.
If you knew, you'd tell me
they were the last nail on your coffin,
& if I believed that were true, I'd have made it four.

I've never been the kind to self-medicate.
Not like you with your afternoon beer that would pour into six.
White cocaine lines cross-stitching your wounds closed
until you'd pick them open again
with that boy-with-fly curiosity.
But I saw nothing wrong with a little men-ication.
I needed to know that not all men were you.

There was Paul 1:
A journalism graduate seven years my junior.
Not much to write home about except for
a cute tagline at the bar—
clever enough to reel me into bed.

Paul 2:
Had a crush on me since high school.
Ever since we went to the formal together
& he bought me a watch. Ironic,
considering I had little time for him.
I made time.

Paul 3:
Yes, I know.
But he wasn't your friend. Not really.
An acquaintance at best.
But he held me afterwards in bed

instead of checking his phone,
& for a moment I sat
on the cusp of you & him
considering taking
the leap into his arms.

It's funny if you think about it:
how being fucked emotionally by one man
only makes you crave
to be fucked physically
by a different one.

THE WAKE UP

Photographs scatter across the floor
like confetti. The battery of my phone
as dead as you. Like huddled mourners
the bedroom walls lean in. I let them hug me.
Fold in on me like a cardboard box.
I hear my heart shatter. The final break.
The box marked *Fragile: Do Not Break.*
Too late.

Your service was eight hours.
I am exhausted by you.
Overwhelmed by the beauty of you,
as I honoured you; paying my respects
to a love that deserved it.
I wish you could've been there. But it's over now.
We only had a lover's fate.
Our goodbye was not "See you again."

I crawl into bed drunk on your side,
filling in the dark empty space you left
like paint spilling colour,
knowing that if you ever come back to me now,
you will be just a ghost haunting me.

I'll light the sage. I'll close my eyes.
Tell myself I'm imagining things.
That perhaps I imagined it all.

RUINS

They never found me in your ruins.
They searched high & low for me,
but I was not recovered.
I never recovered.

I sailed down the river on a single wave.
Falling into a heap of bones
like driftwood on an island shore,
too heavy for the sea to carry.

I knew not what to make of myself.
Shapeless, I had to re-build myself from scratch.
My limbs like firewood
as I sat cross-legged for months,
rubbing two together like thoughts
trying to make sense of myself.
I felt a flicker of warmth.
A warmth that wasn't yours.
A sign that there was life still in these bones.

There was a spark. Then there were many.
I became a fire. I became a flame.
My smoke spinning in circles,
no longer spelling your name.

I am myself now.
The me without you.
Made from amber light,
quiet, & new beginnings.

PARALLELISM

I bumped into your ghost at the mall.
Two shopping bags hanging either side of you
like a slack-armed Jesus;
a crucifix of cigarettes behind your ear.
Face drawn like a child's stick figure.
A sagging around your chin.
As though when my love didn't fill you,
you became a deflated version of yourself.
A balloon the day after the party ends.

The party ended,
& now we're hungover,
maudlin with the realisation
we may have just woken from the best night
of our lives—never to be repeated.
Though not for lack of trying.

Maybe in another life we'd put on
different background music.
Maybe we'd wear our parts to the left,
stop trying to be right.
Maybe we'd invite new friends over.
Ones who were healthier.
Ones who left at a decent hour.
Ones who gave us time to rinse the wine glasses
before bed, scattered across the patio
like offerings to the sun god.

Maybe this time you'd prefer me on top, instead of under.
Maybe this time you'd stroke my hair gently
instead of pulling at it. Or maybe we'd fall into
our usual moulds: your legs straight, mine bent,
my arm curved & limp across your chest

like your cock exhaled against my thigh,
& we'd sigh the kind of sigh
that fooled the world
into believing we were happy
& told us again, we were not.

GESTALT

This strange room.
Pictures hung like dreams
I no longer dream.

Your roaming cat that still won't come to me,
not even with the coaxing of food.

The rest of your things put away in boxes:
your philosophy books
your old strung-out guitar
your love letters.

The air, quiet & anticipating,
sitting upright
like a teaspoon
in an empty sugar bowl.

And I swear I saw your ghost
sitting in the armchair
as I leaned over to pick up your things,
but I couldn't say for sure.

It never dared look at me.

FLINCH

If I meet you in another life,
I'll still flinch.

You'll be a thunderstorm.
A splitting tree.
A black widow spider.
A stranger cutting me off at the lights.
A fist.
A red-tongued flame.

You'll still be danger.
Just with a different name.

NO MAN'S LAND

Folding hope into squares,
I rolled grief on its side.
Tucked my heart between two pairs
of cotton knickers. Zipped my last words shut
like a mouth I wouldn't open
until I arrived.

Moving on was like origami.
Changing shape. Outsmarting geometry.
The creases between my eyes
the only evidence of who I used to be
& which life was harder.

Once I was a paper crane
sturdy & simple on two legs.
Then I was a paper plane,
my wings outstretched, unfolding corners of
the world I'd never seen.
Got more stamps in my passport
to make 90's stamp-collector kid-me jealous.
Laid on ocean shores in Greece.
Rode wobbly lines in Amsterdam.
Let Swiss valleys of flowers breathe me in.

When you left my sight,
there were only places left to see.
Not people.

You were the love of my life.
I had no one else to go.

PICASSHOLE

Like a Renoir painting:
soft strokes & romance,
I loved you like art.
No one was luckier than you.

But you preferred something abstract.
Something more obscure.
The kind of love two strangers would stare at
& argue over its interpretation.

"I don't think they're lovers at all.
    I think they used to be."

"See the way she looks at him—
    & he, like she could be his therapist?"

"Look at his hand on the top of her shoulder.
    That's not comforting. That's annihilating."

You loved like Picasso.
In pieces. Each cubic square of you
opposing.

Crooked.

It's been five years since I buried you.
Each year I tell our story.
Each year I'm stuck on a different page.
I sit in a different chair. Look out a different window.
See things in our story I hadn't seen before
like the branch of a cherry blossom tree peeking
through a neighbour's fence, like the face of a pretty girl
begging to be admired.

Then I see things I used to like,
but no longer do. Like the shade of windowsill
that doesn't match the door.
It bothers me.
It bothers me in a way it shouldn't.
Like the way toothpaste would drip down your shirt
& make me smile,
seeing you as a five-year-old child.
Now it only reminds me of the way I would mother you.
Holding myself accountable for every foolish thing you'd do.

"Why would you still send him things?" they ask.
        "It's nothing," I say. "It's just some things
he might like. A song. A picture of a sunset.
A dried wildflower. He is a ghost. A memory.
People lay flowers on graves.
I lay poems."

NOSTALGIA-NESTHESIA

It breaks my heart
in a way
I can't feel it

& I was just smiling a moment ago
at a funny thing that was spoken
so I know it can't be frozen—I heard it

like a crack from a tree
splitting on a yard a block away
& I thought

Oh, there it is. It still breaks.
My heart still breaks because of you.

Only now it breaks
in a way
I can't feel it.

Printed in Great Britain
by Amazon

41866175R00057